Messy Church® is a registered word mark and the logo is a registered device mark of
The Bible Reading Fellowship

Text copyright © Lucy Moore 2013
The author asserts the moral right
to be identified as the author of this work

Published by
The Bible Reading Fellowship
15 The Chambers, Vineyard
Abingdon OX14 3FE
United Kingdom
Tel: +44 (0)1865 319700
Email: enquiries@brf.org.uk
Website: www.brf.org.uk
BRF is a Registered Charity

ISBN 978 0 85746 116 2

First published 2013
10 9 8 7 6 5 4 3 2 1

Acknowledgments
Scripture quotations taken from The Holy Bible, New International Version® Anglicised, NIV®
Copyright © 1979, 1984, 2011 by www.biblica.com, Biblica, Inc.® Used by permission. All
rights reserved worldwide.

Every effort has been made to trace and contact copyright owners for material used in this
resource. We apologise for any inadvertent omissions or errors, and would ask those concerned
to contact us so that full acknowledgment can be made in the future.

A catalogue record for this book is available from the British Library

Printed and bound by CPI Group (UK) Ltd, Croydon, CR0 4YY

Messy Celebration

Make the most of your

Messy Church celebration time

Lucy Moore

In loving memory of my father, Les Hall,
whose joyful life and faith played a big part
in the making of Messy Church. Party on, Dad.

Acknowledgments

Thanks to the BRF Messy Church team, whose endless treasure trove of ideas I have plundered mercilessly, and to all who generously send in accounts of their Messy Churches.

*

Contents

*

Introduction

Celebrate (verb)
1 publicly acknowledge (a significant or happy day or event) with a social gathering or enjoyable activity (www. oxforddictionaries.com)

Have you ever asked yourself why it's called a 'celebration' rather than a 'service' in Messy Church?

Here's another thought. This is a reflection—by someone else—on a celebration that was visited as part of a gathering of information about different aspects of Messy Church. The report was full of praise for what the local team was doing until it came to the celebration:

For me, the one weak point was the 'celebration', which was far too like a family service. There were too many songs (including churchy words) and a talk (albeit with a visual aid and short) rather than a story. The floating candles for prayers were good, but not easy for everyone to see. Interestingly, some of the families who came halfway through were invited in 'to join the worship'... No wonder they said 'No, thank you' and just waited outside!

I wonder how you react to this. Reactions might include: 'I thought a celebration at Messy Church was *supposed* to be like a family service?' 'How can you avoid "churchy words"?' 'Surely a talk is far better than a story?' 'How can we make sure that everyone can see in a building like ours?' 'What were the team *supposed* to invite the latecomer families to?'

And here's another point to ponder, leading on from that: what did Jesus mean by his challenge to put new wine in new wineskins, and are we at a 'new wineskins' moment?

Neither do people pour new wine into old wineskins. If they do, the skins will burst; the wine will run out, and the wineskins will be ruined. No, they pour new wine into new wineskins, and both are preserved.
MATTHEW 9:17

In the context of the Gospels, Jesus seems to be saying that the traditional religious practices have their place, just as old wine is stored appropriately in old wineskins and probably tastes much better from them. (Does goatskin work like oak casks and give the wine a pleasant tang of goat leather? I cherish my ignorance.) But alongside this, Jesus challenges the religious leaders that there need to be new frameworks to contain the new order he's bringing, just as energetic lively wine will not only be uncontainable in delicate old wineskins but will be destructive and wasteful of wine *and* wineskins. If you have ever witnessed a ginger beer plant exploding in an airing cupboard, you will appreciate the cataclysmic level of chaos that can be wrought by misplaced alcohol.

Are we prepared to change?

'But that was 2,000 years ago!' you cry. 'Surely Christian worship has settled into a safe, mature, predictable formula by now?' Well, no. Sometimes I wonder if the anxiety over altering acts of worship is because we worry that it may seem as if we think God is changing and we know God doesn't change (Malachi 3:6). We may also want organised religion to be an unchanging rock in a rapidly changing world, but that is to mix up the God we worship with the worship we give him. Worship needs to change, or it risks creating cliques of worshippers while losing touch with non-members.

If we take seriously the image of Jesus as the 'living water' (John 4:10), not to mention the 'living bread' (John 6:51) and the 'living stone' (1 Peter 2:4), we can expect our expressions of living worship that reflect this lively God to change constantly over the centuries. I hope Messy Church celebrations will continue to change over time as we try out new ways of enabling gathered worship: that's why in this book you'll find more principles to explore than rules to follow. God seems to have given us in Messy Church a new way of being church, with abundant new life coming in through the door and abundant new faith being nurtured in old and young alike; this is something alive, lively, 'quick', fizzy, full of energy, as unpredictable as a toddler at a birthday party.

Is the celebration an inadequate version of 'real church'?

And that's the problem: what happens if we view our Messy celebrations as simply second-best mini traditional family services and treat them as if they were happening on a Sunday morning? We will end up frustrated because the pattern of worship many of us have on a Sunday depends for its dynamism and shape on having four times as long to take over the service. A shortened version is always going to feel second-best, just as watching a pared-down half-hour version of *Hamlet* is going to lose much of its beauty and drama and risks leaving the audience feeling that Shakespeare isn't much cop.

If we try to pour our Messy congregation into a curtailed form of worship based on a traditional service format, it may mean that the actual format of the celebration and its necessarily short length, passivity, wordiness and rushed delivery puts people off ever trying out Sunday worship (the equivalent of bursting the wineskin). We need to turn our view topsy-turvy and look at the 'problems' of the celebration as *opportunities* to do something new. Both new and old have their place across the beautiful rainbow spectrum of the Church, but it takes discernment to know what precious parts of our worship traditions we can usefully retain in Messy Church without blowing the whole thing through the airing cupboard ceiling.

The Lord says: 'These people come near to me with their mouth and honour me with their lips, but their hearts are far from me. Their worship of me is based on merely human rules they have been taught.'
ISAIAH 29:13

It needs humility to accept that we can't just apply our old patterns of worship to this new situation; that we need to sift through what we have inherited and work out what is valuable, what can be re-imagined and what can be set aside. But it's exciting to reflect that we might be at a point in history where God and the Church have given us the opportunity to reinvent how we worship, not doing something new in a gimmicky or heedless way, but wisely, prayerfully and expectantly in response to this new group of people God has sent to us.

It is not, and never has been, a case of telling traditional church to change the way worship services are organised (although some churches are finding their traditional services being influenced by their Messy experiences); rather, it's about having the freedom, permission and resources to play, to risk, to pioneer in this new congregation. Yes, we will fail and we will get things wrong, but that's what pioneers do. My fear is that as I am pretty steeped in traditional forms of worship myself, this book may not actually be radical enough and may cramp your creativity.

If the invitation came directly from God to re-imagine the celebration in your Messy Church, what might you start doing differently?

'See, I am doing a new thing! Now it springs up; do you not perceive it? I am making a way in the wilderness and streams in the wasteland.'
ISAIAH 43:19

So be affirmed! You and your faith, understanding, delight in God and spirit of servanthood, and your Messy congregation old and young, are all an important part of a new movement of God. This movement is bubbling up in unexpected places and through unexpected people to help grow God's kingdom and bring more and more people to the love, security, hope, purpose and identity of belonging to a church, even if that church looks different from the churches that were around 50 years ago. It's not *the* new movement of God, by any stretch; it's one of many for our time: what an exciting era in which to be a Christian!

We have found that centring everything around tables has worked for us. When families arrive, activity things are set out on eight tables and covered with a cloth while everyone has a welcome drink and biscuit. Activity leaders remove the cloth at about 4pm and we find that people soon settle to different craft activities. We try to have an outside activity when the weather is fine. When a cross appears on the screen, those leading an activity clear away the materials into their crate, and place a cross and candles on their table. In this way we move into a short celebration, which takes place while we are still at the tables. We finish with the Messy Grace, the crosses and candles are put away, and tablecloths and cutlery are put on the tables. Food is brought to each table.
IVY PEACOCK, WOOTTON MESSY CHURCH

*

What is the celebration?

The celebration is a 15- to 20-minute element of gathered worship within a Messy Church session, usually coming after the welcome and the hour of activities and before the meal. It usually consists of a story, song and prayer, but may also occasionally include baptism, Holy Communion or confirmation.

Of all the parts of a Messy Church, the celebration seems to strike most fear into the hearts of the people who are selected to lead it. Do any of these comforting words make the prospect any easier?

You're simply sharing the God who loves you and whom you love with people you love and who love you.

Many adults there will be thinking, 'Thank goodness for [your name]! I couldn't do it half as well as that!' Many children will be thinking, 'I wish I could be [your name]!'

God is right beside you to nudge you the way he wants things to go and to bring good out of even the most apparently disastrous celebration.

The celebration is only one part of the whole Messy Church learning and worshipping church experience.

God wants you to do well. The whole team wants you to do well. Every family wants you to do well: you're all on the same side.

You're giving families a safe space, a place and a shape in which to encounter the risen Christ, something they may never have experienced before.

You're demonstrating that you don't have to be perfect to approach God: 'Look! Even I can do it!'

Where else are these families going to be encouraged to articulate feelings and beliefs about God this month?

You have the privilege of lighting flames of imagination, creating memories and provoking awe, wonder and delight.

At the lowest common denominator, you're providing a church service where nobody tells anyone off...

It may be helpful at this point to list some of the things that the celebration *isn't*.

The celebration isn't a time-filler while the tables are laid up for tea, but a crucial part of the balanced diet of worship that makes up Messy Church.

It's not the one chance for 'proper teaching', but one means of learning among many others across the two hours.

It's not the be-all and end-all of the worship that takes place at Messy Church, but a different complementary expression of worship to add to the mix of encounters with God over the two hours.

It's not a school RE lesson that needs to say, 'Christians believe that...' but a gathered act of worship by a community of believers that demonstrates what we, as that Christian community, believe and gives everyone a chance to experience worship whatever their beliefs.

It's not a lesson or talk that pulls out a moral from a Bible story and presents it pre-packaged and pre-digested, but a life-giving encounter with God through his word that can and should evoke awe, wonder, surprise, puzzlement, questions, anger, joy, laughter or comfort and result in lives transformed.

It's not children's worship, but rejoices in being for all ages. It's not a throwaway that can be led without preparation, but a privileged opportunity to take families from one spiritual dimension to another.

What's the theological underpinning of the celebration?

A healthy instinct

Back when we were planning the very first Messy Church, we always knew we wanted to include a time for gathered worship. I can't honestly remember our stated reasons for doing so. It was something instinctive or perhaps learned from inherited church about feeling that we had to provide an opportunity for explicit gathered worship or we weren't going to be a church at all, just a family craft club.

We always knew it would be hard to tell the story clearly during the craft activities and that we needed a time to make sure everyone had really had a chance to hear the Bible passage of the day. We knew that, people being what they are, it would be easy for some to avoid the activities that involved exercising the spiritual muscles, and that there needed to be a time when spiritual exercise was the only option.

A parallel situation might be a meal: if you put every food item out at the same time, some people might choose only to eat the cake. Parents might find it difficult to insist that their child eats healthily in that setting. A healthier option, and one that would better support a parent in their determination to do the best thing for their child, would be to have a time when everyone was expected to eat carrot sticks, cheese and tomatoes before going on to whatever they fancied, healthy or not. (This is not to reduce the Messy craft time to the status of sweet snacking, as we're seeing so much healthy spiritual development happening through the craft time, but having a celebration as well does ensure a varied spiritual diet.)

After nine years of Messy Church, can we see more reasoned theological underpinning than 'a vague sense of it being the right thing to do' coming out of the practice? I think so.

Worship

This is what the Lord says: 'Let my people go, so that they may worship me.'
EXODUS 8:1B

A great many things can stop people worshipping God. It doesn't have to be slavery to the Egyptians; it might be past experience, preoccupation with demanding children or demanding parents or teachers, tiredness, embarrassment, fear, lack of interest or engagement, hurt... a whole weight of shackles and handcuffs that keep them away from God. One job of Messy Church is to 'let people go so that they can worship God' and the whole of a Messy Church session helps with this.

Remember, and keep remembering (in other words, keep putting those limbs dismembered by habit and staleness back together and breathing breath into the dry bones) that Messy Church is *all* worship from the moment people walk in to the moment they leave (and maybe even that's too limiting). The celebration is *not* 'the worship bit', as we often hear it described. Worship happens over the whole two hours through the welcoming hospitality of all God's people; the gathering of his people; the loving consideration for others as activities are chosen, prepared and presented; the inspiration, creativity, questioning, conversation, relationship and exploration they encourage; the spontaneous confessions and outbursts of praise, awe and wonder that are expressed in conversations throughout; the enjoyment of God's Holy Spirit gently nurturing and healing people around the activity and meal tables.

The 15-minute celebration is a significant element of this liturgy, but works because of its context. It depends on the surrounding elements of hospitality and creativity to have an impact. I am often asked, 'How much teaching can possibly go on in such a short time?' My answer is, 'Very little teaching, but an *enormous* amount of learning *across the whole two hours*.' The brevity of the celebration is its strength. It's different from a traditional church service, which is longer and as a result has a different structure.

While it may be tempting to think that we're being more worthy by talking and singing for longer, there really is a good reason for keeping it short: it's not the only point at which worship is happening, and the learning and worship that have been happening joyfully in the other elements could find themselves deflated, crushed or destroyed by a long, heavy, directive celebration. While worship and learning are distinct, they are related, especially with Messy congregations who have the humility to know they have a great deal to learn; and with children's spirituality, one element of which is the surge of mystery and joy at learning something new. In other words, worship and learning, exploration, discovery and stepping into the unknown are very closely linked.

Growing disciples

Messy Church is in the business of growing disciples, and part of that process is helping people of all ages to learn how to worship God. Would the best way to learn to worship be to sit down with a book about worship and read it through? Or to have a talk about worship from an expert? It's common sense that the best way to teach people what worship is about and how to do it is not to talk about it but simply to worship with them, modelling worship to them and having the grace to let them model new ways of worship to us. We need to be ready to answer any questions that worship provokes in them, but that's easily done.

Whether we're talking about growing child disciples or adult disciples, the best way of learning to worship is by getting on and doing it together: showing a child how to pray in different ways by praying alongside her in different ways; showing an adult how to seize a story by the scruff of its neck and shake the truth out of it by doing that very thing together; showing a family group how to pray together by making space for doing just that in the celebration; putting words to unarticulated feelings; and shaping a theology in songs and prayers that are taken out into bath-time at home or into a tough situation at the office.

The celebration is also an opportunity to grow disciples by encouraging different people to lead all or part of it. In one Messy Church in the Midlands, the youth group took charge of the celebration and were fully responsible for it, which gave them the chance to practise leading worship in a safe and supportive environment. In another Messy Church, the usual suspects weren't available to lead the celebration, so another member of the team tentatively volunteered her services. This not only gave her confidence in her own abilities but demonstrated to the congregation that the job of leading was not only done by those who were perceived to be experts, but by someone just like themselves. Giving the shy but willing teenagers part of the prayer to lead, giving a starter musician a song to accompany using only B flat on their brand-new clarinet, giving someone not used to public speaking a story to tell: all these involve taking a risk, but help people grow in service and confidence and demonstrate the shared identity and responsibility of being a church.

Community

God usually calls his people to be a *community* of people who are freed to be more fully themselves by virtue of living in community, rather than individuals living holy lives in isolation from each other. The celebration and meal—the gathered times of Messy Church—give the opportunity to come together as the family of God after the more disparate activities pursued in the preceding hour. We have been working in (messy) parallel; now in the celebration we are drawn into a circle of belonging. The fact that most people are there as members of a nuclear or extended family group enhances this sense of a celebratory gathering of the tribe, a monthly festival or family party, an expression of the identity of God's people.

Perhaps God has always called his people into community because that way we reflect something of the Trinitarian God who is himself a community: three persons, the same yet gloriously different. Perhaps it's the way Christians learn to love their neighbour, by knocking up against people who are different in age, gender, outlook, financial situation and more. When we have learned not just to put up with each other but to find a way of loving one another in our gathered worship, it's so much easier to love people outside the Church, which is our real job.

Perhaps it's also an expression of the justice and new order of the *ecclesia*, which is one of the words for gathered church used in the New Testament. Whereas in Roman society only men of a certain status and wealth who were nationals would be allowed to join the local *ecclesia*, or gathering, in the radical kingdom of God, the new *ecclesia* is open to absolutely anyone of any age and social background, whether they're a criminal, a child, have special needs, are foreign or *even*… a female.

Perhaps this emphasis on community is to do with a virtuous circle of serving the community in community to bring about the kingdom of heaven on earth, in order to serve the community more so that the body of Christ is built up even more. Paul advocates this in Ephesians 4:11–12: 'So Christ himself gave the apostles, the prophets, the evangelists, the pastors and teachers, to equip his people for works of service, so that the body of Christ may be built up…' We need to give people an experience of gathering as the people of God without levels of seniority or perceived worth, but just coming together as loved and valued children of a loving Father.

Relationships

Closely related to 'community' is the idea that the celebration is an opportunity to foster healthy relationships. This is true of every aspect of Messy Church, and in the celebration the emphasis may be on growing a relationship between each family and God which then deepens the relationships within the family itself as they share an experience that may become a family habit, then a family characteristic, then part of the family identity. There is a value in the shared experience of gathered worship, the sense of not being in isolation, of touching other people's lives and being of value to them. The relationships we create and enable echo the all-accepting love of God for his people. As we understand more of one, we understand more of the other—another virtuous circle.

Something bigger

One of the gifts of the celebration is the chance to communicate openly the message that we've been exploring, sometimes implicitly, through the activity time. The Bible story shows every time that you are part of something bigger than just your own self or your family unit. The celebration states clearly, if non-verbally: 'You are part of a bigger story, God's story. You are significant at a cosmic level. You matter so much that this wonderful man who is also God went to the cross for you and your life can now be wrapped up in the power of the resurrection that eventually turns every messy situation into a happy ending.'

Space

Another gift that the church can give people is that of *space* in crowded, noisy, busy lives, and it is in the celebration more than anywhere else in Messy Church that we can gift-wrap this present and offer it. We often (not always) have a large and beautiful building to meet in, and that sacred space is one that people of all ages appreciate, sometimes because it's so different from the other more prosaic spaces they encounter in the rest of life. In the celebration itself, space is created for silence, listening and reflection—a chance to let go of the reins.

I visited one Messy Church when I was going through a very hectic time with work and found myself simply relaxing into the space the leadership created for listening, relaxing, simply 'being', sitting back for once and allowing other people to take charge. I know worship shouldn't always be a case of letting go of responsibility, cares and critical faculties, but on occasion—especially for tired parents and grandparents— it can be very refreshing. Space created by the tempo and length of a song, space created by the actions of a prayer, space framed by the narrative flow of a story, space that comes from being asked to 'sit down with the people you've come with today', or just the space that comes from being given a time and a place to encounter God: the celebration gives an opportunity for people of all ages to find space.

Guidelines that may be helpful for planning the celebration

We've already thought about the need to have new wineskins for new wine, so it would be totally inappropriate to lay down hard-and-fast rules about what should happen in the celebration. In five years' time, the situation may be completely different and another type of wineskin may be needed. *'Goatskin is so yesterday, darling—have you tried this vegan recycled carrier bag wineskin?'* We wouldn't dream of dictating or prescribing how a celebration must be; we will continue to offer suggestions through resources such as the *Get Messy!* magazine, but you are the experts for your own situation. The only hard-and-fast rule we can lay down is that we all need to stay open to the Spirit of God working in us and in the families we celebrate with as the years pass.

In the book *All-Age Worship* (BRF, 2010) there's a useful list of touchstones for those planning and leading worship with all ages present. You won't make every touchstone apply to every element of every celebration, but you can use them as a checklist to remind you that worship with every age present needs to be distinctively different from the way many of us have been brought up to worship in church. The touchstones are:

- Short, simple
- Senses, symbol
- Space, imagination
- Pattern, participation

Short: Avoid the temptation to sing with endless repetition, to use long, static, one-voice prayers, or to think that you need to give a long talk to make it somehow more worthy. Keep everything short. (Unless the cooking team sends in a panicky message that the pasta hasn't cooked yet and can you please hold everyone in church a little longer...) The people at Messy Church are bravely putting their toe in the terrifying ocean that is church, and they need to know that this ordeal isn't going to last an eternity. And time passes very differently when you're listening and simultaneously trying to keep an eye on three children.

Simple: Don't despise the simple truths, the simple stories, the simple basics of our faith. Simple is not the same as simplistic or dumbed down: it's about exploring the essentials of faith. Use simple language that's accessible to everyone. Avoid clichés. Have a simple framework for your celebration that saves you reinventing the wheel every time, while retaining the option of doing something different on the occasions you feel that's right.

Senses: Bring the senses into the celebration as confidently as you've used them in the activity time: touch, taste, sight, sound, smell. People take in vast amounts through their senses rather than through words alone, and every age group can play a full part in this.

Symbol: Like story, symbols can be taken at different levels and interpreted in a variety of ways, which is perfect for a gathering of people of all ages, life experiences and stages of faith. Give them symbols to visit and revisit over the course of the years. Light. Wine. Bread. Cross. Water. Seed. Fire. Tree.

Space: Make space within the celebration for quiet, for prayer, for people's own individual communion with God, for reflection, for conversation. Worship is not the same as high-energy entertainment.

Therefore, since we are receiving a kingdom that cannot be shaken, let us be thankful, and so worship God acceptably with reverence and awe.

HEBREWS 12:28

Imagination: Give opportunities for people's God-given imaginations to take wing. The chances are that you have some people in your Messy congregation whose approach to God is going to be visionary rather than intellectual, but they may never have been given permission to express it. Use story rather than sermon. Use imagery and encourage short times of imaginative meditation, imaginative prayer, song lyrics that conjure up beauty.

Pattern: Human beings are hard-wired for ritual. A simple liturgy that emerges from your own Messy Church helps embed a certain prayer or action into your long-term memory, where it becomes part of who you are. There may be words or actions from the liturgy of your traditional church services that would be appropriate for Messy Church: our Messy Church delights in praying for each other using the words of the Grace, and we have started praying the Lord's Prayer. I found it very moving to have one of the children who attend both Messy and Sunday church next to me one Sunday. She's a pre-reader and was disengaged for most of the service, but when we got to the Lord's Prayer and the Grace, she suddenly spoke them out with huge confidence, relish and ownership.

Participation: One Messy Church leader wrote in an email from Australia, 'My other query is to do with the celebration time, which we need to work on more. How can we get all involved better? Often the adults and older folk sit back and think this is for the kids, instead of all-age involvement.' Resist the urge to make it an 'It's all about me' show. Try to share out the leadership roles: seek the balancing point between doing everything yourself and the opposite extreme of having so many people popping up to lead a two-second item that a) it takes three times as long, b) there's no cohesiveness or sense of unity, and c) there's no sense of forming a relationship between the enablers and the congregation.

Go through the celebration plan step by step and rigorously transform it so that instead of you being centre stage there are opportunities for everyone to take part. This can be through people joining in the story, saying or doing actions for prayers, carrying items that are needed, talking in groups or whatever it takes to involve everyone. It means that you're placing responsibility for their encounter with God into their own hands, not seizing it for yourself. You're sharing the power and authority in a spirit of equality and justice.

Even if not every member of the team has a 'leadership' role, everyone should feel that it's their joint responsibility to make it a success. I was at one Messy Church celebration where the person leading had given out percussion instruments and found that several small children had decided to hang on to their instruments during his talk and 'participate'. None of the team came and helped the leader out of the noisy situation, but left him to deal with it (unsuccessfully) himself. It wasn't malevolence on the team's part, just a fear of putting themselves forward or seeming bossy, but at the team meeting afterwards it was decided that in future, everyone on the team should feel it is their role to take the initiative in similar situations.

It's also worth taking the trouble to think through as a team how much you want to demonstrate that the celebration is a priority for the team. One Messy Church has decided that the whole team will attend the celebration, even the cooks' team, so they down tools for that 15 minutes and join in. Others deliberately keep the 'setting up the tables for food' team to a minimum so that as many as possible can enjoy the celebration. You'll find ideas for getting not just the team but the whole congregation participating in the Story, Song and Prayer sections that follow.

*

Good communication

'Um, right, now, where did I put my notes? Oh yes, here they are. Katie, could you bring up the first slide on the PowerPoint, please? Is this microphone working? Hello? I said IS THIS… oh yes, so it is. Um, whose child is this swinging on the altar rail? Could their mummy or daddy possibly…? Thank you so much. Now, who remembers what story we looked at last time? The three little pigs? No, I think that might have been at school. Yes, that's a lovely haircut. Nobody remembers last time? Oh dear, that's not very good, is it? If you could pop those mobile phones away, mummies on the back row, just until we've finished, won't be long! Now, where was I? Oh yes, last time's story… oops, oh dear, can someone just stop that toddler pulling down that lit candle on top of her little friend…?'

And lo, nobody did hearken unto the rest of Gloria's celebration at all.

Here are some helpful practical hints for leading a celebration if you're feeling terrified.

Remind yourselves whose church it is—God's, and he is in control.
Remember how much you love each person in your Messy Church, how much God loves them, and how you can expect to meet Christ in them.
Remember how honoured you are that the disengaged

teenager/screeching toddler/texting parent/child intent on destroying the flower arrangement is there at all.

Remind yourselves that any one of these people may have been damaged by church in the past and is perhaps, just *perhaps*, giving church one last chance to love them unconditionally.

Plan and deliver the celebration as a team wherever possible, sharing out the roles.

Before you say anything negative while you're leading the celebration, count to 100. Twice. Then smile.

Be a good stage manager and think through the script, stage directions, props, sound and lighting before anyone comes in.

Sort out the sound system. A good sound system will mean that in any noise wars you will always win. In the end.

Don't expect a respectful silence as you might get at a traditional service. If you want silence, you'll need to work for it. But do you always need silence or could you, for instance, simply break into song, start a silent series of actions, take out something totally intriguing and wait with a glint in your eye…?

Choose your battles.

Make the start of the celebration very clear. Don't dribble into the start of the celebration with throwaway phrases and ineffectual actions: make every word and gesture count.

While you are speaking, it may help you to keep your energy up if you imagine you're a dog with a very waggy tail. (Or it may not.)

Talk to the person on the back row as much as to the person at the front; talk to the left-hand side as much as to the right.

Unless you're telling a Godly Play™ story, make eye contact all round the room.

Keep words to a minimum. Small children and tired adults will switch off very quickly if what you're saying is just verbiage, however witty and chatty it feels to you.

Steer the congregation with a respectful but masterful hand and make it crystal clear what you expect them to say or do at every transition point of the celebration. Set the expectations and don't assume anything. If you want people to sit down, tell them. If you want the celebration to end, say it's over.

If you have a really bouncy congregation, you might need to instigate countdown systems to keep control, such as, 'We're going to count down from ten, starting really loudly and getting quieter and quieter until by the time we reach zero we won't be able to hear *anything*. Then we'll pray.' Ask teachers or Scout and Guide leaders for techniques.

How you say and do things communicates more than what you actually say and do.

Remember that time passes very differently when you're leading from when you're a member of the congregation, so make everything as participative as possible. If in any doubt, say and do less yourself and let others say and do more.

Keep everything short. Short songs, short prayers, short stories, short jokes, short explanations, short instructions, short loud or quiet moments… keep everything short. Long doesn't equal holy. Leave them wanting more.

*

Story

In a Messy Church setting, story is good; sermon is bad. I really mean that. That's just how it is. Far more emphasis is given to training in preaching for our ministers than to training in how to tell a good story, but Jesus knew what he was doing when he told the crowds of mixed ages and backgrounds story after story: 'Jesus spoke all these things to the crowd in parables; he did not say anything to them without using a parable' (Matthew 13:34).

Human minds are built for story. We remember stories, we retell stories to each other, we enter into stories with our brain, our imagination and our emotions; they create community and shared experience, they give a pattern for expectations of what life could, can and should be, they transform lives, and they are fun, whether we're old or young. Parents don't settle down next to a child in bed and tell them a bedtime sermon. People in the pub don't (except in rarefied and esoteric circles) swap sermons over a pint. In Messy Church we want to give people portable theology that doesn't just remain in the two hours of Messy Church but goes out effortlessly into the rest of life with them. We long for it to shape their imagination, their attitude to God and others, and their behaviour. We want it to be retold at home and at school so it spreads like yeast in dough. Let's trust the power of the Bible itself and make sure that people have the chance to hear and remember the story from the Bible, not our own second-hand interpretation of that story.

Another aspect of storytelling is telling *our* stories, the stories of God at work in *our* lives. This is important in this context, as Bible stories can be dismissed as fairy stories by people still on the edge of belief, but to dismiss a story about Freda Bloggs' experience of God in her vegetable patch last week, told by Freda Bloggs, is to call Freda a liar, and you've spent the last hour watching Freda patiently and with infinite kindness teaching your hyperactive five-year-old how to knit. It takes real guts to share personal stories about our faith, but it is part of demonstrating that this faith of 2,000 years ago is alive and well today and transforming lives.

We had a session in every celebration for a year or so, when a certain radio series was on air, that we called 'A History of our Faith in 100 Objects'. We had a short blast of music, a dramatic introduction and our team member of the month had just two minutes to hold up an object and explain the story of why this object was significant on their faith journey. The end of the two minutes was signified, whether they had finished or not, with a quick rendition of the 'Loony Tunes' theme on the saxophone and riotous applause. Photos were taken and put in an album. The objects included a Post-it™ note, a bag of Maltesers™, a WWJD wristband, a frogman suit, a map of the Isle of Wight and several other intriguing items.

Ideas for storytelling

The main thing, when it comes down to it, is how much do *you* care about this story? How excited are *you* by it? How important do *you* think it is that other people hear it? If you love the story, that will be communicated at some level without you even trying. If you can't see that it matters, that will be communicated too. A story, like faith itself, is caught, not taught.

People have different learning styles. Some like *seeing* things, some like *listening* and some like *doing*. Try thinking about one of these styles of learning when you plan your style of storytelling.

Make it visual

Every time you are planning a story, ask yourself, 'Can I make this visual?'

Put up PowerPoint pictures that help tell the story. If you haven't got permission for published ones, why not make it more personal and use photos of the crafts that have been made in the previous hour that are pertinent to the different stages of the story? You could photograph the samples or examples well in advance of the Messy Church itself.

Godly Play™ storytelling (www.godlyplay.org.uk) is very visual. Have a box, bag or suitcase of objects that might have belonged to one of the characters in the story to open up together and create curiosity about that character. Or display just one object from the story—a lamp, a coin, a chain, a loaf of bread—to help people to focus and remember what the story is about.

Use simple costume items to turn yourself or others into a visual aid to tell the story.

Make the furniture into scenery.

Make it fun to listen to

Believe it or not, every person is a natural storyteller, you included. Unless you're telling a story that relies on rhyme and rhythm where it really shows if you get a line wrong, you don't need a book or even a piece of paper to hide behind. Tell the story from your heart and you'll find the natural rhythms of speech will work for you. You'll need to practise beforehand, but that's what dogs, mirrors and long-suffering spouses are for.

Use rhyme and rhythm within the story—have a catchy refrain that occurs repeatedly. (Check out the 'House on the Rock' rap from the Barnabas in Churches website—www. barnabasinchurches.org.uk—for an example of this.)

Ask for a response to a name or phrase that occurs repeatedly in the story. ('Each time I say "Goliath", you say "Ooo-errr!"')

Make the most of the fact that you have a large group of people to create sound effects: it gives a great sense of community and shared experience to create a soundscape of a storm… a forest … a desert… a garden… an angry crowd. (Make sure, though, that *before* you start practising the noisy parts you have thought of a way of making it all quiet again.)

Include actions

Therefore, I urge you, brothers and sisters, in view of God's mercy, to offer your bodies as a living sacrifice, holy and pleasing to God—this is your true and proper worship.

ROMANS 12:1

Set out the chairs or other furniture to form scenery, so that everyone is physically entering the story and surrounded by it: a boat, a road through mountains, a prison cell.

Tell the story dramatically and have people spontaneously act it out as you tell it, especially if there are crowd scenes that everyone can join in with at once.

Move the congregation around the building to tell different parts of the story in different spots if a journey is involved.

Give everyone a simple prop to use in different ways throughout the story (see the way Martha's duster is used in *Messy Church 3*, session 2).

*

Song

Worship the Lord with gladness; come before him with joyful songs.
PSALM 100:2

I suspect there may be as many different opinions on music suitable to use in a Messy Church as there are Messy Church leaders. Songs are perhaps the main means by which people will take theology home with them, through the memorable words of the songs we sing, so it's worth deciding what picture of God and articulation of praise to him we want to suggest through the songs. It's also worth pondering the question: do we actually want to sing at Messy Church? Do we need to? Singing is traditionally done in church gatherings, but hardly anywhere else in an older child's or adult's life, so is it an unmissable part of learning to worship or an element that we could justifiably leave out on the grounds that we don't want to make our congregation feel uncomfortable?

The facilitator of a Meet-up of Messy Church leaders wrote:

Near the end of our time, I threw in some thoughts about the celebration and opened up the dreaded music question! The majority response was that they wanted short, repetitive songs that were quick and easy to pick up and not loaded with heavy 'religious' words. Some used YouTube for well-known ones (such as 'Great Big God') and others drew on Out of the Ark or Fischy Music.

Another idea was writing new, Christian words to well-known pop songs, and many said it would be great to have a CD of new songs especially written and tested for Messy Churches.

The case for singing

Singing creates community.

It is participative: everyone can join in, or just listen if they prefer.

Songs are easy to remember, so are the best way of sending truths home.

As Christians we are called to be countercultural, and if music is beneficial to health, learning and emotions, as it has been proved to be, the church should be giving people the opportunity to do it.

It could be seen as an example of children being models of discipleship, as they often love singing together and approach songs uncritically and with joy.

The ability to enjoy music is one of the last things to leave us if we start to lose our minds in old age.

The case against singing

Choral singing happens at football matches, on hen nights and in primary schools, but in very few other places, so people may feel uncomfortable about singing out loud publicly.

The cringe factor of singing for older children and teenagers can be massive.

Many Messy Churches don't have the luxury of a confident and competent music leader.

Many of the Christian songs so far available are unsuitable for all-age gatherings.

Points to consider when choosing songs for Messy Church celebrations

Songs need to be suitable for adults as well as children.
Songs need to be suitable for children as well as adults.
They should be theologically sound, and the range should include an acknowledgment of suffering and sadness as well as joy.
They should have theological content that's worth singing (something more, please, than 'You are a very nice God and we like you').
They should focus on Jesus and stories about him, not just God the Father and creator, as many children's songs do.
There should be an emphasis on community; in other words, 'we' should be used rather than 'I'.
They should avoid religious clichés, or where these are used, they need to have been thought through. The image of God who 'reigns', for example, is a traditional one, but needs rewording for a less religiously literate congregation who may hear it as 'rains' and in any case may not equate 'all-powerful' with 'monarchy' based on their own cultural experience. Singing sincerely about 'God who made the stars and butterflies' can be a big ask of people raised on theories of the Big Bang and evolution. It can be done, but let it be done thoughtfully and sensitively for this context.
In general, try to find songs that can be sung by a congregation made up of everyone from atheists to Christians. 'I fall down on my knees, devote my life to you and adore you with my

whole heart' may not be the best lyrics to use in this context. Where actions are dictated by the words, such as 'Jump for the Lord' or 'Spin around', take into account people with disabilities as well as adults for whom this might be embarrassing or physically demanding, either because they are physically less flexible or because they're holding twin babies and looking after an excited toddler. (Or, cards on the table, if they're like me and loathe action songs and can never work out whether to mirror the person leading them or use a right hand when the leader uses a right hand… oh, the spatial reasoning involved is just too much.)

The songs should echo or at least not contradict the Messy values: being Christ-centred and all-age, with a focus on hospitality, creativity and celebration.

It's worth asking the local school which songs the children already know from collective worship and using those.

Leading songs in Messy Church

It can help to have a song playing as people enter the worship space, so that the atmosphere is created and it's easier to learn the song later.

Decide how many songs to use: three is enough for a short celebration. One or two may be better—less to learn for tired families.

Don't repeat a song endlessly, as we sometimes do in traditional church services. Be purposeful.

Make it as participative as possible: use percussion instruments; have a band made up of anyone willing to have a go; encourage inexperienced people of all ages to help lead the actions.

Use music to make or frame space within a celebration: for quiet prayer, for instance, or during a prayer activity.

Consider different accompaniments: DVDs, CDs, online clips from YouTube if you have the necessary permission, a live band, single guitar or piano, or sing unaccompanied.

Model a new way of leading the singing: consider where the musicians should stand and what style of song suits your congregation best.

*

Prayer

One thing we're trying to do is to encourage people to pray, not just in Messy Church but continually (see 1 Thessalonians 5:17). So we don't want them to learn things from the way we pray together in church that aren't true or helpful, such as:

You can only pray if a priest is there.
You can only pray in church.
You have to be an expert/a very good person/a grown-up/a child to pray.
My children will be prayed for by someone else, not me.
Prayer is boring and you can just switch off.
Prayer is just words/a formula/spells/charms/a mechanical means to manipulate God.

Instead we want everyone to 'taste and see' what prayer is about, learning by immersion in or exposure to a praying community.

What happens if someone arrives early and finds the team praying?

As we've seen in so many aspects of Messy Church, the message that will be communicated about prayer is how important it is and how real it is to the team leading Messy Church. In other words, if the team is made up of people with an expectant, articulate, Spirit-filled prayer life, there is much more likelihood that the rest of the Messy congregation will catch their enthusiasm for prayer and trust in God.

However, all is not lost if your team consists of reluctant pray-ers who are more prayer worriers than prayer warriors, because over and over again we are seeing the team's prayer lives being renewed and revived by seeing the example of the Messy congregation praying with gusto and by the way God is answering people's prayers in and through their Messy ministries.

Interestingly, although I wouldn't be fussed if a Messy Church celebration didn't include singing, I would be calling in OfMess* if there were no praying.

The celebration shouldn't be the only opportunity people have to pray. Many Messy Churches have found that the congregation values an opportunity during the activity time to bring prayers to God in a more individual, private way, or as a family. After a bereavement, one grandmother arrived early and took her grandchildren into the church before Messy Church began to find some peace and space together. Many Messy Churches set up a prayer table, station, wall or tent that simply encourages people to make time to pray; and of course the activities themselves can easily include something to encourage prayer outside Messy Church: a candle holder displaying words from a prayer, a dice with prayer words or prompts on each face, a bracelet or key ring made of beads

---

*OfMess is a mythical organisation, similar to Ofsted in education, with members who go round in pinstripe suits and PVC aprons inspecting Messy Churches and calling them to order where they are failing. Needless to say, it does not and will never exist while there is breath in my body.

reminding us to pray for people or places, a prayer flag with names on, a wipe-clean prayer board, a decorated notebook, a place mat... the possibilities are endless. Decide as a team, too, what you'd like to do about offering prayer for people, some of whom will be very vulnerable. It may be appropriate to have only certain members of the team who are 'authorised', trained and available to pray with people; it may be appropriate for the whole team to feel able to offer prayer for someone spontaneously as the situation arises. It is wise to involve your minister in the decision and make sure that any training needed is put in place. Safeguarding rules apply, of course, whenever children or vulnerable adults are involved in either offering or asking for prayer.

Points to consider for the celebration prayers

Remember:

- Short, simple
- Senses, symbol
- Space, imagination
- Pattern, participation

Use as few words as possible in prayer, and don't let the prayer time become too long.

Use simple words, actions and aids. Remember that you're trying to model prayers that can be prayed at home, not just in church.

Use the senses: put up a picture to gaze at; light a candle; encourage putting hands in water, in sand, in dough; have something to eat such as a different piece of fruit for each part of the prayer; have music playing or a sound effect from the story.

Use symbol: think about having a symbol for prayer that you use over a period of months to signal that the prayer time is beginning and ending: a cross, a candle, a pair of praying hands.

Make space for people's own prayers. Children are *good* at praying and do it naturally. Adults may well appreciate some space to bring their concerns to God or to consider their own relationship with him in a prayer activity.

Be imaginative as you draw prayers from the story you've explored together. Include items from the story: a temple treasury pot to place a prayer in; a loaf or a fish to draw a prayer on; a wall to stick fears on and have them knocked down; a postcard home from a difficult place... Ask yourself, 'How might someone feel a sense of wonder during this prayer time?'

Include ritual prayers so that people have a chance to learn them and own them. The Lord's Prayer, the Grace, St Patrick's Breastplate, a collect from Common Worship are all useful tools in the toolkit we want to equip people with. Refresh them with actions or gestures or set them to music.

Do as little as possible from the front and encourage as much prayer as possible from the congregation. Remember liturgy is 'the work of the people', so let the people do the work, don't do it all yourself. Let go of the power and responsibility and consider yourself more as a director than an actor.

Collect answers to prayer and celebrate these publicly if it's appropriate. Have a book or display for answered prayers or 'We're still waiting' prayers.

Have something that links the Sunday congregation and the Messy congregation through prayer: a prayer board, access to the emailed prayer cascade, or something like a prayer tree in church that all congregations can use to pray for each other. Try to include teaching about prayer in drip-feed form rather than expositions on a huge doctrine of prayer. Use simple casual comments like, 'We can pray to God anywhere at any time,' 'Prayer is listening as well as talking,' 'I pray for my friend George every time I drive past that gym on the corner.'

Prayer resources and ideas

Invite adults and older children to take digital photos or movie sequences that they can compile on a suitable computer programme (such as Windows Movie Maker). They might be used as the visuals for a song to be played during the prayer time.

Give everyone something related to the theme to hold during the prayer time: a confetti heart, a foil cross, a seed, a person shape (can easily be cut in great numbers on a die-cutting machine). Take care that small children do not put things in their mouths.

Paper shapes sharply folded will open up slowly when placed in water: flower petals, butterfly wings, bird wings, book shapes, hands are all possibilities. Write or draw prayers on them, then fold and place in the water.

Blow bubbles for joyful prayers of thanks or praise, calling out something to praise God for as each one is popped.

Write prayers on a piece of paper, make into a paper plane and simultaneously throw them high, then collect someone else's and pray it with your family or take it home with you to pray this month.

Whisper your confession/sorry prayer into a paper bag and

blow into it, then, on the count of three, pop it to show how Jesus makes our sins disappear.

Write the names of people to pray for on a paper shape that echoes the theme of the day: a cross, a teardrop, a water pot, a candle, a rope, a prison cell.

Make up a simple three-move sequence of arm or hand movements to use in prayer: for example, words of praise with hands up high; words of confession with hands together; words of intercession with hands cupped together and held out.

Use the visual aids around you in your building to pray in different ways. You could move to each one of them if numbers permit. For example:

- Cross: sorry prayers or thank you prayers
- Font: sorry prayers or prayers for people on their Christian journey
- Table: thank you prayers for fun and food around tables
- Stained-glass window (depends what's on it): thanks for the Bible or for saints who have gone before us, or use the colours to pray for people going through different emotions at this time (blue = sad; red = angry; green = jealous, and so on)

Pray using songs as the framework: use words or images between each verse to pray for different situations or people.

Devise a fun or thought-provoking way of bringing the prayers to a close: a Mexican wave or a round of applause, a short quiet verse of a song or the ring of a bell.

Pray in small groups as well as all together.

Use the prayer time as an opportunity to help people reflect on their own relationship with God.

Here is an idea that Alison Thurlow, from Bristol, has successfully used in her Messy Church:

Stick a long strip of white lining paper to the floor at the front of your meeting place. At the far left-hand end, write 'Just looking' in bold letters and draw a pair of glasses; in the middle, write 'Asking lots of questions' and draw a large question mark; at the far right-hand end, write 'I'm a friend of Jesus' and draw some smiley faces. You have now made a sort of continuum to use for your prayer activity. Give each person a small paper figure and a piece of Blu-Tack. Put on some quiet worship music in the background and invite each person to come and stick their figure in the place on the continuum that best represents where they feel they are at this time. Encourage parents to talk to their children and help them to decide where to stick their figure. Finish by praying that God would bless everyone, wherever they are in their faith journey.

If you use this idea, you could photograph the end result and repeat the same activity six months later to encourage people to talk about whether there has been any change in their attitudes.

You'll find more of Alison's ideas on the Messy Church website under 'Faith milestone prayers'.

*

Sacraments

For the past school year, every week during term time, we have had a Messy Mass after school on a Wednesday. In terms of 'Messiness' we are rather simple compared to most—we normally only have a couple of activities on offer, because of our limited resources and the fact that we're doing it every week. Our food and drink is at the end, and again is very simple—just what people happen to bring!

Throughout the liturgy, we move around the church, and I have consciously made sure that everything is interactive, from the entrance where we all light candles, to the songs (to which people can contribute not just by playing instruments but by adding their own words), to the confession (where we dip our hands in the font), to the offertory, and so on.

KAREN GARDINER, ELSTREE

It's very difficult to write about something that has become so emotive and where attitudes vary so much from church to church. The importance that we will each give to sacraments in Messy Church really does depend on where we're coming from liturgically, and there is no 'right' answer to the question 'What part should sacraments play in Messy Church?'

Messy Church embraces all denominations and therefore all shades of the church spectrum need to be respected. Hanging my (loosely low Anglican but with sympathies in many ecclesiastical directions) colours on the mast, I personally believe that Communion is one of the gifts Jesus has given us to help us to get to know him better, to 'taste and see that God is good'. I don't believe that it is the pinnacle of Christian worship or the ultimate measure of Christian maturity or invariably the most helpful element of someone's walk with God. I believe that Messy Churches that do not offer Communion services are just as much 'church' as Sunday morning Eucharistic congregations, but that Communion is a rite that links us with Christians over the last two millennia and across the world, and is an unambiguous sign of belonging to the kingdom. Communion expresses as nothing else does our unity with and in Christ, and can help nurture our faith and understanding. My personal view (continued) is that a Messy Church of any denomination should be open to the possibility of offering Communion.

My sense is that you will know if and when it's appropriate to offer a Messy Church session centred around Holy Communion, and that there's no need to rush or worry that you're not there yet. After all, until relatively recently, most churchgoers in the UK would only have had Communion on high days and holidays. The same applies to baptism and confirmation: you will know when it's right to offer them.

How might a Messy Church approach the sacraments, particularly those of Holy Communion and baptism? We can do no better than go back to the Messy Church core values: creativity, hospitality, celebration, being all-age, being Christ-centred.

Holy Communion

So we think about Holy Communion…

… in a spirit of creativity

Imagine you have carte blanche to lead a Communion service exactly as you think it should be done for your Messy congregation, old and young, baptised and unbaptised. What would you do?

Imagine what it's like never to have been in a church before. What is it like for a child or an unchurched adult to approach Communion? Put yourself in their shoes. How can you ensure that it is full of mystery and connects us with a numinous God, rather than baffling, boring, exclusive or frustrating? What aspect of it needs exploring before someone of any age can understand enough of the actual ceremony to feel a connection?

Imagine using the shape of Messy Church to reinforce the theme. Instead of making Messy Church fit standard liturgy, how might the shape of a typical Messy Church enhance the shape of Communion? Can you creatively use all the elements of Messy Church to make it a holistic experience? For example, using formal words of greeting in the welcome time; intentionally including confession, intercession and scripture in the activities, with perhaps a handout that guides everyone round the different activities and explains how they fit into the whole. Should the meal happen before or after the celebration? Or could the sacrament happen around the activity or meal tables?

Imagine using the building creatively. How might your building help you with this celebration? Its shape, its furniture (fonts, tables, stained glass, side chapels or simply doors, tables, chairs, floor)?

Imagine the participants' roles differently. How might the congregation of Messy Church contribute to the celebration? Could they create a form of greeting, invite people to worship, devise prayers, join with the minister in blessing the congregation, in distributing the bread and wine, in other parts of the celebration?

Imagine the impact of a whole year of exploring the Eucharist. A Messy Church keen to explore the richness of the Eucharistic imagery might try holding a Communion in every celebration over a year, with a different aspect of Communion and faith explored in each:

1) Bread, grain and yeast
2) Wine, vine and cups
3) Tables, hospitality, feast
4) Body of Christ, unity, community
5) Servanthood
6) Cross, sacrifice
7) Justice, freedom and kingdom of heaven
8) Alpha and omega, beginnings and endings
9) Remembering

10) Healing and reconciliation
11) Hope, Christ coming again
12) Trinity, presence of Father, Son and Holy Spirit

... in a spirit of hospitality

Communion is perhaps the most vivid illustration of Jesus' hospitality, feeding his guests with his very self, inviting everyone to his table, not because they have earned a place there or deserve a place there, but longing for everyone to come: 'Come, all you who are thirsty, come to the waters; and you who have no money, come, buy and eat! ... Listen, listen to me, and eat what is good, and you will delight in the richest of fare' (Isaiah 55:1–2).

We can offer this hospitality that makes sense of Galatians 3:28: 'There is neither Jew nor Gentile, neither slave nor free, nor is there male and female, for you are all one in Christ Jesus.' Everyone can come to the table. It isn't the inner sanctum or the top table at a feast to which only those of privilege and high status are invited, but a table for everyone regardless of status, gender or age, a table of justice and equality.

A problem may arise for Messy Church when we go to the verses before this, which unavoidably put a limit on the hospitality by stating that the expectation of unity comes from baptism: 'So in Christ Jesus you are all children of God through faith, for all of you who were baptised into Christ have clothed yourselves with Christ' (Galatians 3:26–27). This might imply that some of the church in Galatia weren't yet baptised or clothed with Christ, so perhaps Paul had the same issue of deciding who receives Communion. For many of our congregation, baptism is still a long way off, so how do we make them welcome at God's table before then?

People can learn a great deal about Communion and feel part of the occasion without taking Communion, but simply by being present. Most Messy Churches have a mixture of adults who are baptised and those who aren't; of children who are baptised and those who aren't, so it won't be a case of the 'churchy people' receiving bread and wine while the others don't; it will be a real mixture of ages and faith backgrounds who take Communion or don't. The hospitality will be revealed in the words and manner the minister uses to explain what s/he expects people to do when it comes to the distribution.

You can also express hospitality in your consideration for those who can't yet read: try to do as much without printed words as possible. Make it as inclusive and egalitarian as possible. Stand around the table if possible, rather than sitting in rows in front of it. Hospitality is two-way, so make every opportunity for the celebration to be as participative as possible, everyone playing their part, sharing out the roles, working together for and with each other.

... in a spirit of celebration

We 'celebrate' Communion. There is food and drink! There are other family members! Let the celebration chime with the 'feel' or 'flow' of the whole Messy Church and echo the party-like nature of the atmosphere you've created in the activity session. In other words, don't suddenly go dull, pompous, churchy or staid. Allow the drama of this wonderful story to come to the fore. This doesn't mean disrespectfully, but rather by showing it matters. Don't feebly waft a wafer: rip apart a huge loaf of bread. Don't pick up the wine casually: *show* it to everyone, *make* them notice it. Use your energy, your body, your voice, language, music, colour, visuals, scents and movement to draw out the drama, engage people and make the celebration memorable.

You can also let the celebration flow on into the meal that follows it by making it clear in your sending out that you're sending them out to the next part of the Communion, perhaps referring to the way the first Christians would share the bread and wine of Communion in the context of a meal. Perhaps you could invite them to say a line from the Communion service as they sit down to eat, emphasising the integrity of the whole Messy Church session. 'The gifts of God for the people of God' is one possibility. Perhaps you could simply have baskets of bread and jugs of blackcurrant juice waiting on the tables and allow them to make their own imaginative leap.

... being all-age

I think this is more a case of emphasis than content, but do whatever you can to help families come to the Lord's Table as families, not as individuals. Make explicit the invitation to come or pray or do the actions 'with the people you came with today'. Ensure that the way you're organising it includes elements for and from adults and for and from children. Include everyone from the youngest to the oldest, and actively make sure you don't exclude anyone.

... being Christ-centred

Help people to make the link between the Jesus they learn about and meet every time at Messy Church and the Jesus of the story of the Lord's Supper: in other words, make sure the ceremony doesn't overshadow the person. It might be as simple as introducing the story of the Last Supper with a reminder of the sort of things Jesus said and did so that it is clear who is at the centre of this celebration. The Communion is then a logical progression from the other stories about a person we know and love rather than an experience with no points of reference.

Baptism

I just want to share with you one of our joyous moments of Messy Church… In September we had a 'Messy Communion', which was very successful. We talked about being baptised, then shared Communion. Two boys, twins, said they hadn't been baptised and went away to think it over with their family. On 27 November we had a most wonderful Messy Church first real baptism! We, the team, were so proud and the boys were so excited. We had a table of food, drew around our hands and put the outlines on a tree to represent a warm welcome to our family of St Andrew's. Altogether 51 people enjoyed this joyous service of baptism.
CHERRILL JAMES, ST ANDREW'S, KEGWORTH

One function of the big 'special occasion' sacraments like baptism or confirmation is to link the participants to the wider Church, so there's no absolute need to celebrate them in the Messy Church itself, although if that's what the families are happy with, that's wonderful and affirms that your church really sees Messy Church as 'real church' in the broader picture.

At the end of January 2011 we held a Messy Church with a difference. Five children took Communion for the first time, three people affirmed their faith, two were baptised and ten were confirmed. I should just say that we'd been talking with people about this service and encouraging adults to take responsibility for their faith in a variety of ways for a while. Everyone who came to this service did know it would be different and longer!

The key pressures came from balancing the need of the Bishop to follow the law of the Church of England and our wish to make the service accessible and understandable for the majority of the Messy Church congregation who are either children or have no or little experience of formal church.

At the rehearsal we realised that only one person knew what 'the peace' was. Things that church regulars take for granted, prayers that they know by heart, are unknown territory for most Messy Churchers and could easily divide the congregation in a service—which is exactly what we do not want in Messy Church.

We pared the service requirements to the bone, chose the shortest Communion Prayer and then added opening and closing prayers that were in everyday but very meaningful language; trying hard to keep the theology of the occasion without dumbing down or making it so simple it was meaningless. We wanted this to be a memorable time for all those involved—in a good sense!

The service sheet, more of a book really, included absolutely every word and instruction. This meant that everyone could take a full part on an even footing. We made sure there was a regular churchgoer at the front whom you could follow if you got lost, and said so in the welcome.

We moved everything we could out of the 'service' section—like the prayers—and into the 'activity' section that comes first; trying to shorten the service without losing any of its meaning or worship elements. The children brought forward, as they often do, a collage of all our prayers written on paper cut-outs of our hands and glued as feathers on a dove—Come, Holy Spirit!

We're still smiling at the experience and wondering when we can do it all over again!

REVD DR J.M. WHITE, RECTOR OF ALL SAINTS' CHURCH, WINGERWORTH

(You can read the full story in the Messy Blog of 28 November 2012.)

＊

Beyond the celebration

Celebrating into the mealtime

Given that the celebration is an integral part of the worship of Messy Church, why not try extending the theme not just into the craft activities before the celebration but into the mealtime afterwards? You could put something on each meal table to give families an excuse to think further about the story they've just heard or the ideas that came to them. We sometimes put 'Scribble Sheets' and pencils on each table. They have just two questions for the table to discuss and scribble answers for, such as 'What did you like best at Messy Church today?' and 'When did you feel closest to God today?'

At the Messy Church of BRF team member Jane Leadbetter, in Liverpool, L19, there is a short walk between the church building where the celebration takes place and the hall where the meal is held. The team were worried the theme would be forgotten on the way, so they decided to have question cards on each table prompting people to think about the celebration. Some families now demand the question cards as soon as they sit down and take great pride in filling in thoughtful answers. In the 'Table Talk for Messy Moments' game (www.tabletalk.org) there is a pack of cards specially designed for use on the meal tables in response to any theme.

Celebrating at home

One of our aims with Messy Church has always been to resource, enable and encourage parents and carers to take responsibility for their family's faith, rather than, as has so often been the case in the past, to leave the whole responsibility to the church and to see the gathered faith community and its 'experts' as all that's needed for a full life of faith. We want to help families to take the celebration they have experienced in Messy Church out of gathered church and into their homes. It's about 24/7 faith, de-professionalising faith, giving permission for faith to be expressed to suit the needs of individual families rather than 'one size fits all', and sharing with justice and equality: a sign of the kingdom.

As you plan your celebration, be thinking, 'How can we model aspects of worship in the celebration that families can take home and use there?'

Take-home sheets are one obvious way of doing this: providing an easily achievable low- or no-cost idea with the suggestion 'To try at home'. Even if it takes many months before a family tries it out, at least you've sent out the message that the families have permission to do it, that there's some sort of expectation that they could do something independently of gathered church, that they can create church in their home in a small or big way. It's one way of demonstrating that all believers are priests (1 Peter 2:9). In *Messy Church 3* and the *Get Messy!* magazine there are take-home ideas with every session that can be used or adapted, or you can create your own based on your knowledge of your families.

Another idea is to send home a very simple liturgy (words and actions) for a seasonal celebration: a Christingle that can be made, talked about and sung around at home; a retelling of the Easter story using an Easter garden you've made together at home; a re-enactment of the Last Supper with questions such as a Jewish Seder meal; a nativity set through which the story can be played out; a simple summer thank-you liturgy to say round a sandcastle on a beach on the theme of the House on the Rock, or a barbecue liturgy on the theme of fire; a prayer to share on the first day of term; or a birthday ritual that includes God. Such a script might be a duplicate of the one that you have used at Messy Church.

The things you make during the activity time may also be a means of encouraging celebration at home. The section on Prayer above has some ideas. You might also build on the way children learn by playing and re-enacting stories, and make something that helps them 'play' the celebration story at home: a matchbox with tiny objects from the story; one key life-sized object from the story; a set of picture cards that tell the story. One four-year-old went home from our last Messy Church and demonstrated to his dad how the lantern he had made 'shines out light like Jesus shines out through people': the object had given him the excuse to replay and retell the theme. You might have an activity where you make a set of question cards for meal tables at home like the ones you use at Messy Church. Or, if you hold a baptism, you might make a baptism set of a small model font or bowl that holds water, a tiny person, a tiny minister and a model candle: you can imagine children replaying the baptism at home to explore what happened in the church, and a parent being enabled to play along or to explain and reflect more on baptism in the process.

*

And to finish...

I asked at the start of this book why we call it a 'celebration' rather than a 'service'. For the first Messy Church at St Wilf's, it was the result of thinking what would appeal to our new congregation, not calling it a 'service', which might have connotations from the past of boredom, duty or religiosity ('I don't do religion' is a phrase we often hear from Messy Church adults), but a 'celebration', which is about joy, fun, community and significance.

Perhaps most importantly, the celebration is one of the four elements in a Messy Church session that give everyone a chance to encounter a life-changing God. We put out our Scribble Sheets on the meal tables and asked, 'What did you like best today?' and 'When did you feel closest to God?' *Every* element of Messy Church featured in *both* sets of replies: the welcome, the activities, the celebration and the meal. The celebration 'works' because of the other parts of Messy Church; the other parts 'work' because of the celebration.

So let's not sell the celebration short. Let's not treat it as 'church lite' or a substandard, watered-down version of traditional services. Instead let's build on the freedom of being a new form of church and see the apparent restrictions—the limitations of time, the range of ages, the lack of preconceived ideas about worship, the low attention threshold, the urge to move and be loud, an inability to read, the presence of many children—as strengths and gifts and an invitation from our loving God to think afresh about how we can create celebrations that help more people of all ages come close to him.

Yet a time is coming and has now come when the true worshippers will worship the Father in the Spirit and in truth, for they are the kind of worshippers the Father seeks.
JOHN 4:23

*

Further resources

Resources for worship with all ages

Going for Growth website, www.going4growth.org.uk

Storytelling resources

Creative Ways to Tell a Bible Story, Martyn Payne (Barnabas for Children, 2013)
The Gospels Unplugged, Lucy Moore (Barnabas for Children, 2011)
The Lion Storyteller Bible, Bob Hartman (Lion Hudson, 1995)
You will also find some great stories and free articles about storytelling on the www.barnabasinchurches.org.uk website.

Music resources

Fischy Music (www.fischy.com)
Out of the Ark (www.outoftheark.co.uk)
Jim Bailey (www.jimbailey.org)
John Hardwick (www.johnhardwick.org.uk)
Doug Horley (www.duggiedugdug.org)

Prayer resources

Multi-Sensory Prayer, Sue Wallace (Scripture Union, 2000)
Creative Ideas for All-Age Church, Karen Bulley (Barnabas, 2010)
Dan's Tool Box (www.bristoldiocesecyp.org)
www.engageworship.org

Other Messy Church resources from BRF

Available from your local Christian bookshop or direct from BRF: visit www.brfonline.org.uk

Get Messy!

Get Messy! is a four-monthly subscription resource for Messy Church leaders, featuring a wide range of contributors from the Messy Church in-house team, including Lucy Moore and Jane Leadbetter, and Messy Church teams around the world. Each issue contains four session outlines (one per month), including handout sheets, take-home ideas and a planning template, together with information on the latest resources and events. It also seeks to encourage and refresh Messy Church leaders by providing monthly Bible studies, inspirational articles and a problem page. Other features include a youth column, a day in the life of a Regional Coordinator and stories from Messy Churches around the world.

Enjoyed

this book?

Write a review—we'd love to hear what you think.
Email: reviews@brf.org.uk

Keep up to date—receive details of our new books as they happen.
Sign up for email news and select your interest groups at:
www.brfonline.org.uk/findoutmore/

Follow us on Twitter @brfonline

By post—to receive new title information by post (UK only), complete the form below and post to: BRF Mailing Lists, 15 The Chambers, Vineyard, Abingdon, Oxfordshire, OX14 3FE

Your Details
Name _____
Address_____
_____
Town/City _____ Post Code _____
Email_____

Your Interest Groups (*Please tick as appropriate)	
❏ Advent/Lent	❏ Messy Church
❏ Bible Reading & Study	❏ Pastoral
❏ Children's Books	❏ Prayer & Spirituality
❏ Discipleship	❏ Resources for Children's Church
❏ Leadership	❏ Resources for Schools

Support your local bookshop
Ask about their new title information schemes.